WACKY INVENTIONS THROUGHOUT HISTORY

Weird inventions that seem too crazy to be real!

Written by Joe Rhatigan
Illustrated by Celeste Aires

TABLE OF CONTENTS

THE CRAZIEST CONTRAPTIONS

Inventors are dreamers who come up with creative solutions to problems or new ways to do things. Some of these inventions are wonderful and life-changing. Others are not very helpful at all. And others are really incredibly wacky.

This book is about the wacky ones: the boat cars, the lawn mowers, and the wearable radios. Some of these inventions exist as actual products people can buy. Some were never built because they were just too weird. But at one point, each of the wild wonders in this book was thought up by someone who wanted to earn some money and perhaps also make the world a better place.

Enjoy this trip through the wacky world of gadgets and contraptions. Maybe one of these will lead you to come up with your own awesome (or weird) invention!

SIMPLY ALARMING

The problem with alarm clocks is that people ignore them and oversleep anyway. Inventors have been trying to solve this problem for years. The time-alarm bed invention solved the problem, but caused a different one. It didn't just set off an alarm when it was time to get up. If you didn't act quickly, the bed also tipped sideways, tossing you onto the floor. Yes, it woke you up, but it could lead to injury (or at least a grumpy start to your day).

DID IT WAKE UP THE WORLD?

The time-alarm bed was invented by George Seaman way back in 1892. It didn't become popular; people decided it was better to be late than be thrown to the floor every morning.

CATCHER'S CAGE

Catching a fastball can hurt—even when you're wearing a glove. And the gloves used in the early 1900s didn't provide much protection. While baseball players and inventors worked on creating bigger and better gloves, inventor James Bennett tried something different. He came up with a catcher's cage. With this loony device, catchers simply let a pitched ball hit them in the chest, where the wire cage "caught" it and then released it through a hole in the bottom.

DID IT CATCH ON?

Bennett tried for years to get players and investors interested in his cage, as well as his idea for a two-handed catcher's glove. But gloves, known as *mitts*, were simply much easier and more comfortable to use.

SOMETHING FISHY

This 1920 invention is a wearable submarine. The giant fish head goes over your own head, leaving your arms free and your legs in two rubber tubes. Inside there's a motor and an air storage tank. Simply put the suit on, turn on the engine, and... most likely sink to the bottom of the ocean.

GREAT MINDS THINK ALIKE

Seabreacher is a company that manufactures diving machines in the shape of whales, sharks, and fish. These powerboats look like jet-fighter sea creatures and can race across the water, dive, and then jump out again, like a dolphin or whale.

SOGGY DOGGY

It's a fact of life: dogs get dirty. Also, many dogs absolutely hate taking baths. That's why students in Thailand invented a machine that acts just like a canine car wash. Place your pet in the contraption and press some buttons. Warm, sudsy water sprays the dog clean while brushes move back and forth over and under the dog. A few minutes later, the dog comes out sopping wet—and clean.

GREAT MINDS THINK ALIKE

A French inventor created the Dog-O-Matic, which looks a little too much like a washing machine—thankfully without the spin cycle. This invention also blow dries the dog after the bath.

H2 GO!

It's a car! It's a boat! It drives! It floats! Beginning in 1961, Americans were able to buy the Amphicar Model 770, a car that was also a boat. Was it a very good car? Not really. Was it a reliable boat? No. But that didn't stop nearly 4,000 Amphicars from being built and sold. The Quandt Group in Germany stopped making the vehicle in 1967. People just didn't need a car that swam. That's what bridges are for.

HISTORICALLY HYSTERICAL

President Lyndon Johnson owned an Amphicar. He liked to give people rides and scare them by driving into a lake. The president would yell, "The brakes don't work! We're going in!"

POWERED BY PAWS

Z. Wigg was an 80-year-old retired railroad worker when he decided to invent a new way to both get around town and walk his dog. He created a vehicle with a giant hamster wheel in the center for the dog to walk in. When the dog walked or ran, the giant wheel turned, which engaged a belt-and-pulley system that moved the back wheels. This unique dog walker also had a steering wheel and headlights.

WAS IT TOP DOG?

No dog is going to be happy about being trapped inside a big wheel. And the power a walking dog creates isn't enough to move this crazy contraption quickly or far. Plus, what if you have a Chihuahua?

THE WEED WACKY

The Wonder Boy X-100 was invented in 1957 by Simplicity Manufacturing. This crazy contraption took a simple problem—cutting the grass—and solved it with a space-age, air-conditioned mower that would look more at home on Mars. This goofy golf cart promised to cut the grass, vacuum the lawn, spray weed killer, and plow snow. Meanwhile, the operator worked from the comfort of a domed control center that even had a telephone.

DID IT MAKE THE CUT?

Some inventions seek to make doing chores easier or more comfortable. Sometimes, like with the X-100, they overdo it. Called the "Lazy Man's Power Mower," this invention was never made. That's probably because it should have been called the Crazy Man's Power Mower.

THE HAT-IO

In the 1940s, radios were as big as TV sets. That didn't stop sixteen-year-old Olin Mumford from inventing one of the first radios you could take with you. He created this radio helmet because he wanted to listen to his favorite shows anywhere. This radio hat included headphones, vacuum tubes, batteries, dials, and a giant antenna.

DID ANYONE TUNE IN?

Olin and his invention got some attention in newspapers. But his radio hat didn't take off because it was too heavy. Once the transistor was invented a few years later, portable radios became all the rage.

FULL OF HOT AIR

Wouldn't you love having a robot that cleaned your room and took you places? Robots may seem like modern inventions, but people have been creating different kinds for more than 150 years. One of the first was the Steam Man. It was invented and built in the 1860s, before electricity. It had a small engine and boiler in its chest that moved the robot's legs so it could pull a carriage. Steam came out of the robot's top hat.

HISTORICALLY HYSTERICAL

The Steam Man could supposedly travel a mile a minute. However, it had trouble on rough dirt trails or other uneven surfaces. Some reporters at the time questioned whether it even worked at all. It probably didn't! But its invention did lead to some of the first science fiction stories about robots. And it started the robot craze that continues to this day.

A WHEELIE BAD IDEA

Early car inventions were modeled after horse-drawn carriages, which had four wheels. In the early 1930s, Dr. John Purves wondered whether or not we could simplify things and just drive a wheel. He invented the Dynasphere, a giant, 10-foot-tall, doughnut-shaped wheel car that held a driver and three passengers. Step inside the wheel, start the engine, and hope you don't get a flat!

DID IT TAKE OFF?

While the Dynasphere drove up to 30 miles per hour, it couldn't steer (you had to lean one way or the other), go, or stop very well. And if you were really unlucky, there was a chance the driver and passengers would spin head over heels like a hamster that stops running in its wheel.

TRIKE 'N' MOW

Most people want to keep their children away from sharp blades. But the inventor of this lawn mower tricycle would rather the kids help out in the garden. This three-wheeled toy/grass cutter was invented as a quiet and gas-free solution to loud and smelly gas mowers. Also, parents could enjoy their quiet home while their loud and smelly kids worked away outside.

DID IT MOW DOWN THE COMPETITION?

Although finding a greener way to cut the grass while getting some good exercise is a wonderful idea, nobody wanted their kids to lose their fingers and toes for a well-kept lawn.

ROCK-A-BYE BATHTUB

In the 1890s and early 1900s, people thought moving and splashing water was healthy, so many rocking bathtubs were invented and sold. One problem was that water always ended up on the floor. This invention solved the splashing problem by creating a "drape" that went all the way up to your neck. Rock away!

TELL ME MORE!

Rocking bathtubs were meant to mimic the movement of rivers and oceans. This treatment was supposed to increase blood circulation, calm the nerves, and cure many diseases. Psst...it didn't do any of those things.

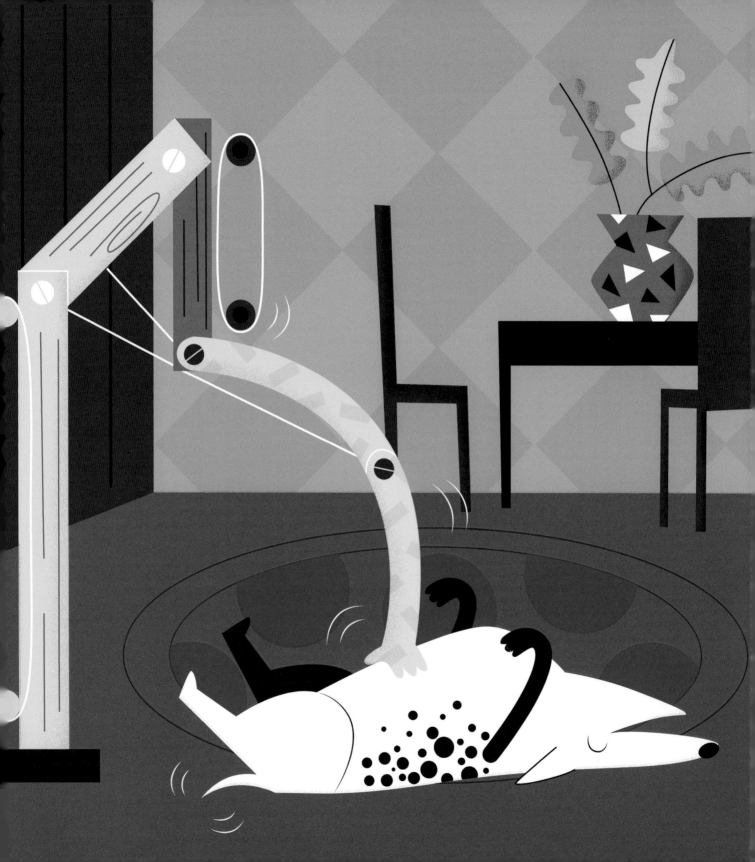

HEAD SCRATCHER

Do you worry about your dog while you're at school? In 1989, inventor Rita Della Vecchia created the Pet Petter—a mechanical arm and hand that does the petting while you're away. Your dog walks to the device and waits for it to turn on. In a moment, your pet is being petted and scratched as if you were there. Maybe now your pooch will stop eating your shoes!

TELL ME MORE!

According to the patent application, the arm would be fully adjustable to handle any size dog. Simply raise or lower the arm to custom fit your pet. The petter would also include an "electronic eye" that senses when your dog is in the right position and ready for some love. Sadly, this invention is still in the planning stages.

OH, BUOY!

Back in the 1870s, the inventor Traugott Beek thought of a great way to keep people afloat and alive in case of a shipwreck. His life preserver was a suit made of waterproof canvas and metal rings. You raised it over your body, closed the hood, and floated away. Inside, you could enjoy food, water, and a little bit of wiggle room as you waited to be rescued. Meanwhile, the metal rings protected you from sharp rocks and sharks.

DID THIS IDEA FLOAT?

There is no evidence that this lifesaving device was ever actually built. Why not? Well, for one thing, how did it float? A person's body weight, along with the metal rings, would most likely sink this strange-looking costume.

This library edition published in 2019 by Walter Foster Jr.,
an imprint of The Quarto Group
6 Orchard Road, Suite 100
Lake Forest, CA 92630
© 2017 Quarto Publishing Group USA Inc.
Published by Walter Foster Jr.,
an imprint of The Quarto Group

Written by Joe Rhatigan
Illustrated by Celeste Aires

Distributed in the United States and Canada by
Lerner Publisher Services
241 First Avenue North
Minneapolis, MN 55401 U.S.A.
www.lernerbooks.com

First Library Edition

Printed in USA
9 8 7 6 5 4 3 2 1

MIX
Paper from responsible sources
FSC® C008080

Also available in this series:

978-1-942875-69-7   978-1-942875-70-3   978-1-60058-788-7   978-1-60058-789-4   978-1-60058-801-3   978-1-94287-571-0   978-1-94287-572-7